D1017232

YOU'RE OLD AF.

Here's a book (because it's
not like you go out any more)

summersdale

YOU'RE OLD AF

An Hachette UK Company
www.hachette.co.uk

Summersdale Publishers Ltd
Part of Octopus Publishing Group Limited
Carmelite House
50 Victoria Embankment
LONDON
EC4Y 0DZ
UK

www.summersdale.com

Printed and bound in China

ISBN: 978-1-78783-000-4

Substantial discounts on bulk quantities of Summersdale books are available to corporations, professional associations and other organisations. For details contact general enquiries: telephone: +44 (0) 1243 771107 or email: enquiries@summersdale.com.

To...

From.....................................

I HAVE THE
BODY OF AN
EIGHTEEN-
YEAR-OLD.
I KEEP IT IN
THE FRIDGE.

Spike Milligan

'OLD AF' MEANS 'OLD AND FABULOUS', RIGHT?

YOU KNOW YOU'RE OLD AF WHEN...

you go to the pub for 'just one', have just one, and are in bed at a reasonable hour.

MIDDLE AGE
IS WHEN
YOU'RE FACED
WITH TWO
TEMPTATIONS
AND YOU
CHOOSE THE
ONE THAT
WILL GET YOU
HOME BY NINE
O'CLOCK.

Ronald Reagan

I DON'T PLAN TO GROW OLD GRACEFULLY. I PLAN TO HAVE FACELIFTS UNTIL MY EARS MEET.

RITA RUDNER

'WELL, BACK IN MY DAY...'

AGE IS JUST A NUMBER. A BIG, FAT, EVER-INCREASING NUMBER.

_____

THE ONLY
REASON I
WOULD TAKE
UP JOGGING IS
SO THAT I COULD
HEAR HEAVY
BREATHING
AGAIN.

Erma Bombeck

**Experience is
a comb life gives
you after you
lose your hair.**

JUDITH STERN

YOU KNOW YOU'RE OLD AF WHEN...

your most interesting topic of discussion is what you've brought for lunch. Spoiler: it's hummus.

AGE IS SOMETHING THAT DOESN'T MATTER, UNLESS YOU ARE A CHEESE.

Billy Burke

ANOTHER DAY, ANOTHER DISGRACE.

THE SURPRISING
THING ABOUT
YOUNG FOOLS
IS HOW MANY
SURVIVE
TO BECOME
OLD FOOLS.

Doug Larson

Wine &
Fire &
Blankets &
Chill.

SHUT THE FRONT DOOR! THEN OBSESS FOR HOURS OVER WHETHER YOU LOCKED IT.

I HAVE REACHED
AN AGE WHEN, IF
SOMEONE TELLS
ME TO WEAR
SOCKS, I DON'T
HAVE TO.

Albert Einstein

TO ME,
OLD AGE
IS ALWAYS
FIFTEEN
YEARS OLDER
THAN I AM.

Bernard Baruch

YOU KNOW YOU'RE OLD AF WHEN...

the latest music makes all the sense of a foreign language.

YOU ARE THE PARTY STARTER (AND THE FIRST TO LEAVE).

OLD WOOD BEST TO BURN, OLD WINE TO DRINK, OLD FRIENDS TO TRUST, AND OLD AUTHORS TO READ.

Francis Bacon

PUSHING FORTY? SHE'S HANGING ON FOR DEAR LIFE!

Anonymous

A MOMENT ON THE LIPS, A LIFETIME ON YOUR SURGICALLY REPAIRED HIPS.

YOU KNOW YOU'RE OLD AF WHEN...

a nap goes from being a luxury to a necessity.

THE OLDER I GET, THE BETTER I USED TO BE.

Lee Trevino

I HIGHLY RECOMMEND GETTING OLDER. THERE'S LESS TENDENCY TO PEOPLE-PLEASE.

ALANIS MORISSETTE

SOCKS FOR CHRISTMAS? YES, PLEASE.

Peace &
Quiet &
Alone time.

ANYTHING INVENTED AFTER YOU'RE THIRTY-FIVE IS AGAINST THE NATURAL ORDER OF THINGS.

Douglas Adams

I LOVE
EVERYTHING
THAT'S OLD:
OLD FRIENDS,
OLD TIMES,
OLD MANNERS,
OLD BOOKS,
OLD WINE.

Oliver Goldsmith

YOUR YOUNGER SELF WOULD HATE WHAT YOU'VE BECOME. BUT THAT PERSON IS GONE, SO WHO CARES?

YOU KNOW YOU'RE OLD AF WHEN...

'cheese night' isn't drunkenly dancing to bad tunes, but enjoying brie from a board and admiring your neighbour's extension.

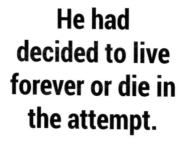

He had decided to live forever or die in the attempt.

JOSEPH HELLER

THE SECRET OF STAYING YOUNG IS TO LIVE HONESTLY, EAT SLOWLY AND LIE ABOUT YOUR AGE.

Lucille Ball

YOUR UGLY
SWEATER
COLLECTION
ISN'T EVEN
IRONIC.

I'M SORRY —
THIS MUSIC
IS SO LOUD I
CAN BARELY
HEAR HOW
FANTASTIC
YOUR LIFE IS.

THERE IS STILL NO CURE FOR THE COMMON BIRTHDAY.

John Glenn

MIDDLE AGE IS WHEN, WHEREVER YOU GO ON HOLIDAY, YOU PACK A SWEATER.

Denis Norden

YOU KNOW YOU'RE OLD AF WHEN...

the word 'cool' comes out of your mouth as 'lovely'.

THE HAIR-DYE DAYS AREN'T TOO FAR AWAY.

MATURITY IS A HIGH PRICE TO PAY FOR GROWING UP.

Tom Stoppard

THERE IS NO PLEASURE WORTH FORGOING JUST FOR AN EXTRA THREE YEARS IN THE GERIATRIC WARD.

John Mortimer

Avocados &
Tapas &
Brunch &
Vino.

THEY WERE DEFINITELY HERE A SECOND AGO...

YOU ARE RAPIDLY
APPROACHING
THE AGE WHEN
YOUR BODY,
WHETHER IT
EMBARRASSES
YOU OR NOT,
BEGINS TO
EMBARRASS
OTHER PEOPLE.

Alan Bennett

MIDDLE AGE IS WHEN A GUY KEEPS TURNING OFF LIGHTS FOR ECONOMICAL RATHER THAN ROMANTIC REASONS.

Lillian Gordy Carter

YOU KNOW YOU'RE OLD AF WHEN...

you have to be told there's no definite article in 'the iTunes'.

LIFE'S TOO SHORT. EVEN SHORTER, NOW.

WHEN YOU ARE DISSATISFIED AND WOULD LIKE TO GO BACK TO YOUTH, THINK OF ALGEBRA.

WILL ROGERS

THE OLDER I GROW, THE MORE I DISTRUST THE FAMILIAR DOCTRINE THAT AGE BRINGS WISDOM.

H. L. Mencken

PEOPLE CAN'T SAY 'YOU ARE WISE BEYOND YOUR YEARS' ANY MORE.

_____

YOU KNOW YOU'RE OLD AF WHEN...

you visit your friend's new place and excitedly marvel at 'all the storage'.

When I
was a boy,
the Dead Sea
was only sick.

GEORGE BURNS

MIDDLE AGE IS WHEN YOUR AGE STARTS TO SHOW AROUND YOUR MIDDLE.

Bob Hope

YOU KNOW YOU'RE OLD AF WHEN...

you only swipe left and right to clean your windows.

WOW –
WHAT A RED,
SHINY, LOUD,
IMPRACTICAL
CAR!

_____

BY THE TIME
A MAN IS WISE
ENOUGH TO
WATCH HIS
STEP, HE'S
TOO OLD TO
GO ANYWHERE.

Billy Crystal

Jogs &
Yogs &
Tog counts.

TO WHAT DO
I ATTRIBUTE
MY LONGEVITY?
BAD LUCK.

Quentin Crisp

YOU KNOW YOU'RE OLD AF WHEN...

you realise everything you say is just a different breed of complaint.

OLD AGE AIN'T NO PLACE FOR SISSIES.

Bette Davis

MIDLIFE IS WHEN YOU REACH THE TOP OF THE LADDER AND FIND THAT IT WAS AGAINST THE WRONG WALL.

Joseph Campbell

WHEN YOU SAY YOU'RE GOING OUT YOU MEAN YOU'RE GOING OUT TO THE GARDEN.

YOUR OLD PLAYLIST RESEMBLES NOISE RATHER THAN MUSIC.

I REFUSE TO
ADMIT THAT
I'M MORE THAN
FIFTY-TWO,
EVEN IF THAT
MAKES MY SONS
ILLEGITIMATE.

Nancy Astor

MIDDLE AGE IS WHEN WE CAN DO JUST AS MUCH AS EVER - BUT WOULD RATHER NOT.

Anonymous

YOU KNOW YOU'RE OLD AF WHEN...

missing an hour of sleep feels like you've pulled an all-nighter.

CONGRATULATIONS!
YOU'RE A
DAY CLOSER
TO DEATH!

I KNEW I WAS GETTING OLD WHEN THE POPE STARTED LOOKING YOUNG.

BILLY WILDER

YOU CAN'T TURN BACK THE CLOCK. BUT YOU CAN WIND IT UP AGAIN.

Bonnie Prudden

Garden centres & Tea rooms & Hobby shops & Cake.

YOUR WEEKENDS NOW CONSIST OF CLEANING AND CRAFTING.

———————————

I CAN HONESTLY
SAY I LOVE
GETTING OLDER.
THEN AGAIN,
I NEVER PUT
MY GLASSES
ON BEFORE
CHECKING
THE MIRROR.

Cherie Lunghi

Youth is when you're allowed to stay up late on New Year's Eve. Middle age is when you're forced to.

BILL VAUGHAN

YOU KNOW YOU'RE OLD AF WHEN...

there are adults walking around today who were born in a different century to you.

'THAT WAS HR. THEY WANT A WORD ABOUT YOUR "OPINIONS!".'

IF I KNEW I WAS GOING TO LIVE THIS LONG, I'D HAVE TAKEN BETTER CARE OF MYSELF.

Eubie Blake

THERE ARE NO OLD PEOPLE NOWADAYS; THEY ARE EITHER 'WONDERFUL FOR THEIR AGE' OR DEAD.

Mary Pettibone Poole

'ALEXA –
WERE
YOUNG
PEOPLE
ALWAYS
THIS
RUDE?'

YOU KNOW YOU'RE OLD AF WHEN...

you remember the sound that dial-up modems made when connecting to the internet.

WE ARE ONLY
YOUNG ONCE.
THAT IS ALL
SOCIETY CAN
STAND.

Bob Bowen

SO FAR, THIS IS THE OLDEST I'VE BEEN.

George Carlin

WHAT'S THE ONLY THING BETTER THAN A NIGHT OUT? A CANCELLED NIGHT OUT.

Sensible speeds & Sensible bedtimes & Sensible portions & Vegetables.

FORTY IS THE OLD AGE OF YOUTH; FIFTY IS THE YOUTH OF OLD AGE.

Victor Hugo

AS WE GROW
OLDER, OUR
BODIES GET
SHORTER AND
OUR ANECDOTES
LONGER.

Robert Quillen

I'D RATHER
BE DONNING
MY PYJAMAS
THAN PARTY
WEAR.

YOU KNOW YOU'RE OLD AF WHEN...

drinks on a work night are non-existent.

MIDDLE AGE: WHEN YOU BEGIN TO EXCHANGE YOUR EMOTIONS FOR SYMPTOMS.

Georges Clemenceau

EACH YEAR IT GROWS HARDER TO MAKE ENDS MEET – THE ENDS I REFER TO ARE HANDS AND FEET.

RICHARD ARMOUR

I USED TO LOVE RAVES BUT NOW I LOVE HUMMUS.

IF HUMANS AGE LIKE BANANAS, WELCOME TO THE LAST POINT YOU'RE STILL EDIBLE.

I ABSOLUTELY REFUSE TO REVEAL MY AGE. WHAT AM I — A CAR?

Cyndi Lauper

As you
get older, the
pickings get
slimmer, but the
people don't.

CARRIE FISHER

YOU KNOW YOU'RE OLD AF WHEN...

you keep your coat on at the pub like a Sherpa on the side of a mountain.

MIDDLE AGE IS WHEN ANYTHING NEW IN THE WAY YOU FEEL IS MOST LIKELY A SYMPTOM.

Laurence J. Peter

JOKES YOU NEVER LAUGHED AT ARE STARTING TO BECOME FUNNY.

HOW FOOLISH
TO THINK THAT
ONE CAN EVER
SLAM THE
DOOR IN THE
FACE OF AGE.
MUCH WISER
TO BE POLITE
AND GRACIOUS
AND ASK HIM
TO LUNCH IN
ADVANCE.

Noël Coward

Cleaning & Tidying & Cooking & Cleaning again.

IT'S NO LONGER
POSSIBLE TO
REPRESENT
YOUR AGE WITH
THE NUMBER
OF CANDLES
ON THE CAKE —
YOU NEED A
MUCH BIGGER
CAKE FOR THAT.

DON'T WORRY ABOUT AVOIDING TEMPTATION. AS YOU GROW OLDER IT WILL AVOID YOU.

Joey Adams

WISDOM DOESN'T NECESSARILY COME WITH AGE. SOMETIMES AGE JUST SHOWS UP ALL BY ITSELF.

Tom Wilson

YOU KNOW YOU'RE OLD AF WHEN...

someone sends you a Valentine's card and you write back asking for a large-print edition.

YOU COULD TALK GARDENING TO ME ALL DAY.

!

THIRTY-FIVE IS WHEN YOU FINALLY GET YOUR HEAD TOGETHER AND YOUR BODY STARTS FALLING APART.

Caryn Leschen

I'M TOO OLD FOR
A PAPER ROUTE,
TOO YOUNG FOR
SOCIAL SECURITY
AND TOO TIRED
FOR AN AFFAIR.

Erma Bombeck

ADOPTING THE QUIRKS OF YOUR PARENTS IS A SURE SIGN OF GETTING OLD.

YOU KNOW YOU'RE OLD AF WHEN...

you sneakily nudge your alarm to 8 a.m. because it's the effing weekend, yo.

I'M SIXTY-FIVE... BUT IF THERE WERE FIFTEEN MONTHS IN EVERY YEAR, I'D ONLY BE FORTY-EIGHT.

James Thurber

I'M AT AN AGE
WHERE MY BACK
GOES OUT MORE
THAN I DO.

PHYLLIS DILLER

REMEMBER WHEN YOU WOULD HEAR THE WORD 'TEQUILA' AND YOU'D GET INSTANT TRAUMA-NAUSEA.

Plants &
Pics &
Coasters &
Cushions.

THERE'S ONE MORE TERRIFYING FACT ABOUT OLD PEOPLE: I'M GOING TO BE ONE SOON.

P. J. O'Rourke

MIDDLE AGE IS THE AWKWARD PERIOD WHEN FATHER TIME STARTS CATCHING UP WITH MOTHER NATURE.

Harold Coffin

SOME PEOPLE LOOK GREAT FOR THEIR AGE. BUT I'M SURE YOU HAVE OTHER QUALITIES.

YOU KNOW YOU'RE OLD AF WHEN...

you set your alarm early on a Sunday to go to the local market.

We are young
only once.
After that,
we need some
other excuse.

ANONYMOUS

DON'T LET AGEING GET YOU DOWN. IT'S TOO HARD TO GET BACK UP.

John Wagner

YOU HAVE AT LEAST ONE PRESCRIPTION ON REPEAT.

ONE WHIFF OF CHOCOLATE AND YOU GAIN WEIGHT.

———————

THERE IS ABSOLUTELY NOTHING TO BE SAID IN FAVOUR OF GROWING OLD. THERE OUGHT TO BE LEGISLATION AGAINST IT.

Patrick Moore

MEMORY IS THE FIRST CASUALTY OF MIDDLE AGE, IF I REMEMBER CORRECTLY.

Candice Bergen

YOU KNOW YOU'RE OLD AF WHEN...

your pride and joy is no longer your booze collection but your cleaning cupboard.

IN MY DAY
THEY WERE
TWICE AS BIG
AND HALF
THE PRICE.

LIFE WOULD BE INFINITELY HAPPIER IF WE COULD ONLY BE BORN AT THE AGE OF EIGHTY AND GRADUALLY APPROACH EIGHTEEN.

Mark Twain

EVENTUALLY
YOU WILL REACH
A POINT WHEN
YOU STOP LYING
ABOUT YOUR
AGE AND START
BRAGGING
ABOUT IT.

Will Rogers

Chunky knit & Loose fit & Elastic.

I THOUGHT IT COULDN'T GET WILDER, BUT NOW I'VE GOT ANOTHER BOARD GAME TO PLAY ON SATURDAY NIGHTS.

_____

OLD AGE IS LIKE
EVERYTHING
ELSE. TO MAKE A
SUCCESS OF IT,
YOU'VE GOT TO
START YOUNG.

Theodore Roosevelt

I'M OFFICIALLY MIDDLE-AGED. I DON'T NEED DRUGS ANY MORE. I CAN GET THE SAME EFFECT JUST BY STANDING UP REAL FAST.

Jonathan Katz

YOU KNOW YOU'RE OLD AF WHEN...

instead of ignoring the 'clean up your rubbish' notices in the work kitchen, you're pinning them up.

I'M JUST SAYING WE SHOULD THINK ABOUT SEPARATE BEDS.

YOU ARE ONLY YOUNG ONCE, BUT YOU CAN STAY IMMATURE INDEFINITELY.

OGDEN NASH

I'VE NEVER KNOWN A PERSON TO LIVE TO BE ONE HUNDRED AND BE REMARKABLE FOR ANYTHING ELSE.

Josh Billings

YOU WANT TO SEE MY ID? MARRY ME NOW.

YOU OPEN INCOGNITO BROWSER TABS TO SEARCH YOUR LATEST ACHES AND PAINS.

The first sign of maturity is the discovery that the volume knob also turns to the left.

JERRY M. WRIGHT

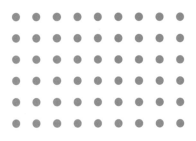

I DON'T SO
MUCH MIND
BEING OLD,
BUT I MIND
BEING FAT
AND OLD.

PETER GABRIEL

STORMZY? ISN'T HE THAT STREET-ART GUY?

Cats &
Cat food &
Cat toys &
More cats.

YOU KNOW
YOU'VE REACHED
MIDDLE AGE
WHEN YOU'RE
CAUTIONED TO
SLOW DOWN BY
YOUR DOCTOR,
INSTEAD OF BY
THE POLICE.

Joan Rivers

THE OLDER YOU GET THE STRONGER THE WIND GETS – AND IT'S ALWAYS IN YOUR FACE.

Jack Nicklaus

RONALDO'S ON HOW MUCH? ALL HE HAS TO DO IS KICK A BALL INTO A NET.

YOU KNOW YOU'RE OLD AF WHEN...

Mrs Doubtfire goes from comedy figure to kind of sexy.

BIRTHDAYS ARE GOOD FOR YOU. STATISTICS SHOW THAT THE PEOPLE WHO HAVE THE MOST LIVE THE LONGEST.

Larry Lorenzoni

THE OLDER YOU GET, THE BETTER YOU GET - UNLESS YOU ARE A BANANA.

Ross Noble

TIMES YOU'VE HAD: BAD TIMES, HARD TIMES AND DISAPPOINTING TIMES. TIMES YOU HAVEN'T HAD: FREE TIME.

I KNOW I'M IN THE KITCHEN. BUT WHY?

I'M STILL
GOING ON
BAD DATES
WHEN I SHOULD
BE IN A BAD
MARRIAGE
BY NOW.

Laura Kightlinger

I'M LIKE OLD WINE; THEY DON'T BRING ME OUT VERY OFTEN, BUT I'M WELL PRESERVED.

Rose Kennedy

YOU KNOW YOU'RE OLD AF WHEN...

mirrors develop this problem where they make you look like a Basset hound.

NOTHING
IS MADE
LIKE IT USED
TO BE.

AGE DOES NOT DIMINISH THE EXTREME DISAPPOINTMENT OF HAVING A SCOOP OF ICE CREAM FALL FROM THE CONE.

JIM FIEBIG

AS FOR ME, EXCEPT FOR AN OCCASIONAL HEART ATTACK, I FEEL AS YOUNG AS I EVER DID.

Robert Benchley

SILVER FOX? MORE LIKE DIRTY PIGEON.

———————————————

YOU KNOW YOU'RE OLD AF WHEN...

you start having to go to the toilet in the night.

**Growing old
is compulsory.
Growing up
is optional.**

BOB MONKHOUSE

If you're interested in finding out more about our books, find us on Facebook at **Summersdale Publishers** and follow us on Twitter at **@Summersdale.**

www.summersdale.com